READ AND CIR

Facts for the People of Michigan!!

STATE AND NATIONAL FINANCES, AND THE KANSAS POLICY OF THE DEMOCRATIC PARTY, 1858.

TO THE PEOPLE OF MICHIGAN.

By the State Central Committee.

In eighteen hundred and fifty-four the people of this State exercised their high prerogative, through the medium of the ballot-box, to repudiate the "Democratic" party, which had so long held control over the financial and general affairs of the State, and placed those affairs in the hands of the REPUBLICAN party. After two years of ardent duty, in which the interests of the State were administered with signal fidelity, the Republican party was again endorsed by an overwhelming majority at the memorable contest of 1856; and the Democratic party, which, with unblushing impudence then sought to be restored to power, was again rebuked and repudiated. Another important campaign has arrived, and the REPUBLICAN party submits its claims for another and third endorsement at your hands. It is with a deep and sincere consciousness of the honest and frugal administration of the interests of the State, by the past and present Republican administration, that your endorsement is again asked, with the fullest confidence that it will be given with cheerfulness and zeal. The Republican party have sought to retain the confidence of the people, in the sterling character of the State ticket which has been placed in nomination to administer the future interests of the State.

The Hon. MOSES WISNER, of Oakland County, enjoys an enviable reputation as one of the most able and profound lawyers and statesmen in the northwestern States. His administration, as Governor, will be wise, just and judicious.

Hon. EDMUND B. FAIRFIELD, candidate for Lieutenant Governor, has already distinguished himself by his learning and ability, no less than by his thrilling eloquence, in the Legislative Halls of the State.

NELSON G. ISBELL, for Secretary of State, and Hon. JOHN MCKINNEY, for State Treasurer, are also widely and favorably known as sound statesmen, in the past legislation of the State, and will be found both "capable" and "honest" in the faithful discharge of any duty imposed upon them. John McKinney has already served the State, for four years, with strict integrity and general satisfaction.

DANIEL L. CASE, of Ingham, is eminently fitted for the important office of Auditor General; while Hon. JAMES W. SANBORN, of St. Clair, will administer the interests of the State in the office of Commissioner of the State Land Office, with a perfect familiarity with all the wants of the people and the State.

The re-nomination of Hon. JACOB M. HOWARD as Attorney General, is a signal evidence that the Republican party will frown upon all *peck*ulations and fraudulent appropriation of money from the treasury, or extravagant and unnecessary expenditures. He is already known as a terror to the former Democratic plunderers of the public treasury, as well as for his eminent legal ability.

The names of JOHN M. GREGORY, for Superintendent of Public Instruction, and WITIER J. BAXTER, Esq., for the Board of Education, are already widely known for their devotion and zeal in the cause of Education and Common Schools; and this important trust cannot be confided to better or safer hands.

The eminent fitness and ability of each candidate upon the State ticket, for the various positions for which they are nominated, not less than the high moral character of the individual, is a strong guarantee to the people that the affairs of the State will be administered with marked frugality, wisdom, prudence and integrity, by the candidates above named, whom we have the fullest assurance will be triumphantly elected, by an honest and discriminating constituency.

Opposed to this judiciously selected ticket, asking for the suffrages of the tax-paying voters of Michigan, is the ticket of the Democratic party, endorsing the infamous *Dred Scott* decision—endorsing the infamous pro-slavery policy of the National Administration, by which the fetters of slavery were sought to be fastened upon our free brethren of Kansas, by a system of force, fraud, perjury and bloodsheed, that has disgraced the administration of James Buchanan and brought a stain upon our national character—endorsing also the attempt of the National Democratic administration to admit a slave State with one-third the population that it required for the admission of a free State; and, furthermore, endorsing the flagrant frauds and peculations upon the State treasury, by which hundreds of thousands of dollars were fraudulently abstracted by Democratic officials, previous to the reign of the Republican party. With singular assurance, and a total disregard of the sentiments of a liberty-loving people, this party, whose leaders have fattened upon the public treasury, by the fraudulent and unauthorized use of the peoples' money, through a long series of years, now again ask to be restored to place, to power, to plunder, and to confidence!! *We have the most abiding confidence that their wishes will not be gratified.* Writhing in all the agonies of starvation, the leaders and journals of the repudiated Democratic party are resorting to the most desperate measures of detraction, in reckless assertions towards the Republican party and administration, to frighten the people into a change of policy.

It is no less with a view to meet these groundless charges, and furnish a complete answer to all these falsehoods, and vindicate the integrity of the Republican administration, by placing the facts before the people, than to exhibit the frauds and maladministration of the Democratic party in past years, that the Republican State Central Committee have deemed it appropriate to issue this document; the facts and information in which are compiled from official sources, and may be relied upon against whatever inventions may be put forth during the campaign.

The frauds upon the peoples' treasury, already discovered, while the Democratic party was in power, are too palpable and glaring to be so soon forgotten or forgiven by the people; while we challenge the utmost scrutiny as to the integrity with which State affairs have been administered by the Republican party, regardless of all reckless and unfounded assertions.

How the Democratic Party made the State Debt.

When the people of the State assumed State sovereignty, the Democratic party being in power, proceeded to encumber the people with a State Debt as follows:

General Fund Bonds, act of Nov. 14, 1835, ...	$ 100,000
Five Million Loan bonds, act of March 21, 1837,.	5,000,000
Penetentiary bonds, act of April 19, 1837,.....	40,000
Palmyra and Jacksonburg R R bonds, June 22, 1837,......	20,000
State Penetentiary bonds, act of Mar. 22, '38,.	20,000
Detroit and Pontiac R R. bonds, act of March 5, 1838,......	100,000
University bonds, act of April 6, 1838,.......	100,000
Allegan and Marshall R. R bonds, act of April 6, 1838,......	100,000
Ypsilanti and Tecumseh R. R. bonds, act of April 6, 1838,......	100,000
Delinquent Tax bonds, 1839,......	31,000
Interest bonds, March 8, 1843,......	363,324
Total Debts to 1843,..............	5,974,324

The bungling and fraudulent way in which the Five Million Loan was managed—the entire bonds being handed over to irresponsible parties before one tenth part of their value had been received—lost the State several hundred thousand dollars, and cost it the charge of "repudiation," among the bond-holders, for refusing to pay the bonds upon which nothing had been received by the State—however much had been received and used by individual Democrats on private account, as in the case of a fraudulent re-issue of bonds in 1854.

Democratic Receipts and Products.

Down to January 1, 1843, received in cash on bonds, and other acknowledged State indebtedness,..		$3 535,334 24
Received of U. S. 500,000 acres of land, worth $1 25 per acre,....................		625,000 00
Total receipts to 1843,................		$4,160,334 24
Products.		
Michigan Central R. R. sold for...	$2,000,000	
" Southern " " ...	500,000	
		2,500,000 00
		$1,660,334 24
Add interest from January, 1843, to 1846, when the railroads were sold, say,.......		339,665 76
Total loss in 10 years,............		**$2,000,000 00**

This was the first exploit in Democratic financeering in our State affairs.

The way they Pocketed the Surplus Interest.

The total receipts into the Treasury for seven years, from 1848 to 1854 inclusive, and the cash balances on hand at the end of each year, were as follows:

1848,......................	$392,693 00	$52,736 98
1849,......................	494,165 06	55,597 47
1856,......................	429,941 92	36,057 85
1851,......................	414,390 18	92,391 21
1852,......................	451,082 97	116,555 21
1853,......................	655,667 86	375,773 68
1854,......................	610,699 97	553,004 08
	3,448,640 96	1,287,116 48

Showing that the annual average of balances for seven years was $183,873 78.

During the three years of Republican administration the annual balances, in cash, have been as follows:

1855,................................	$516,626 13
1856,................................	288,015 77
1857,................................	158,690 33
Total balance for three years,.........	1,063,329 33

Being an annual average of $534,443 11.

Upon this annual average in the hands of the Republican party, for three years, there was paid into the State Treasurery by the present State Treasurer, for *interest account upon the balances*, the sum of **$61,484 55.**

During the seven years Democratic rule, with an annual average of $183,873 78 on hand, they paid into the Treasury, on interest account, the *astonishing* sum of **$1,553 86!!**

Slight difference between Democratic and Republican ratio of Interest.

The rate of interest paid upon the annual balances for seven years, by the Democratic party, was LESS THAN ONE-FOURTH PER CENT! although the law required them to pay *not less* than one per cent.

The rate of interest paid upon the balances for three years, by the Republican party, was OVER SEVENTEEN PER CENT upon the average balance for the average time; and at a ratio SIXTY-SIX TIMES GREATER *than the interest paid into the Treasury under Democratic rule.*

The amount of $73,446 13 withheld by Democrats from the Treasury, in Interest.

Amount due the State on interest account, from 1848 to 1854, by the Democratic party, at the same rate paid by the Republican State Treasurer for three years past, was, say	$75,000 00
Amount actually paid by Democratic party,	1,553 86
Amount retained for private use,	$73,446 14

Being a GRAND AVERAGE of over $10,492 A YEAR FOR SEVEN YEARS!! which went from the pockets of the Tax-Payers into the pockets of Democratic officials, and Democratic leaders, for private purposes!

The Democrats Last Grab—Another $60,000 Gone.

One of the most bare-faced and audacious frauds practiced upon the treasury by the Democratic party, after it had been repudiated at the ballot-box in 1854, was a lot of fraudulent claims, which were dug up and allowed during the last month of their power—in December, 1854—and which they did not put into their last annual report. These were all old exploded claims, which had been often examined and rejected many years before, while the claims, and all the circumstances and facts connected with them, were fresh in the knowledge of former State Auditors and Legislatures.

These fraudulent claims were allowed, as follows:

Dec. 2, 1854 —Gilbert & Co., damages by reason of misrepresentation of the Commissioner of Internal Improvement made to induce a low bidding on letting contract on Clinton and Kalamazoo Canal,	$2,204 29
Phœnix Bank, N. Y., claim for advance of $16,400 on State Bonds delivered Cashier Farmers' & Mechanics' Bank, Detroit, by order of Gov. Mason, for use of the State, March 13, 1838, and interest thereon,	35,603 74
Dec. 15, 1854 —Job Brookfield, second branch of claim, being for expenses and costs of suit in defence of his title to fractional quarter of Sec. 35, T. 7 S. range 17 W., and for depreciation in value of said land in consequence of action of the State,	4,000 00
Bronson, Knight & Ingalls, claim for damages by reason of misrepresentation of Commissioner of Int. Imp., to induce a low bidding on letting contract on Clinton and Kalamazoo Canal,	6,234 78

The aggregate amount of these claims, with the interest to this time, is *more than sixty thousand dollars*, taken out of the money paid into the treasury by the tax-payers of the State, and distributed among those leaders who had access to the State vaults!

The Phœnix Bank claim, thus fraudulently abstracted from the treasury, has been sued for and a judgment obtained, by Attorney General Hon. Jacob M. Howard, and the case is now pending in the Courts of the State of New York. The Bank, wishing to delay payment, has appealed the case from the Superior Court, Judge Hoffman, to the full Bench, where the former judgment will be confirmed, and the money returned to the Treasury.

Another Grab on a Picayune Scale.

A twice paid bill, by the Democratic party officials, for the same work, has been discovered by the vouchers on file. By this picayune grab the treasury, fortunately, was depleted of only $450, which, with the interest up to this date, makes an aggregate of about $675. We simply submit a copy of the vouchers of the transaction, with the remark that the Attorney General has commenced suit, also, for the recovery of the amount.

STATE OF MICHIGAN, To Geo. W. Peck, Dr.

May 7, 1853.—To binding 4,500 copies of Session Laws of 1853, at 10c, ... $450 00

The above is correct.

ROD. R. GIBSON, *Dep. Sec'y of State.*

$450 00. Received of the Auditor General a warrant upon the Treasurer of the State of Michigan, for the sum of four hundred and fifty dollars and..........cents, in full of the above amount. GEO. W. PECK.

Lansing, May 19, 1853.

STATE OF MICHIGAN, To Geo. W. Peck, Dr.

May 7, 1853.—To binding 4,500 copies of Session Laws of 1853, at 10c, ... $450 00

The above work has been done, and the number of copies have been delivered.

ROD. R. GIBSON, *Dep Sec'y State.*

$450 00. Received of the Auditor General a warrant upon the Treasurer of the State of Michigan, for the sum of four hundred and fifty dollars, and..........cents, in full of the above account. GEO. W PECK.

Lansing, Aug. 18, 1853.

FRAUDULENT RE-ISSUE OF STATE BONDS —ANOTHER $3,000 SUNK.

After the Republican party were entrusted with the affairs of the State, it was discovered that the State had been swindled out of the sum of $2,269 40 by the fraudulent re-issue of State Bonds to that amount, which it has been ascertained was used in private speculations by a member of the retiring Democratic State administration. It has also been ascertained that the whole Board of State officials in 1854 were cognizant of the fraudulent transaction; if they did not share in the proceeds. The sum, wtth interest to this time, amounts to about THREE THOUSAND DOLLARS more gone from the Peoples' Treasury.

A FLAT CAP OPERATION.

Among the wholesale swindles discovered by the Republican State officials, which were practiced by the Democratic State officers, was one shown by the following voucher:

AUDITOR GENL'S OFFICE.

To S. D. ELWOOD & Co.,	Dr.
For 315 reams flat cap, 15 lbs, for Tax blanks, 340	$1,071 00
Six boxes,	5 00
	1,076 00

Detroit, Dec 13, 1854.

Received payment. S. D. ELWOOD & Co.

Allowed at $1,076; W. GRAVES, Ch'm. of State Auditors. Correct. O. C. WISWELL, Dep. A. G.

The whole thing was a *deliberate swindle*, from first to last.

Elwood & Co. never delivered a *single sheet of the paper*, and the State never received a sheet of paper as indicated in the above voucher. The Democratic State officers *deliberately paid the amount knowing it to be fraudulent.* Whether the amount was divided between Elwood & Co. and the State officers, the public may judge. The whole amount and interest sunk in this swindle is $1.377 28.

THE COST OF A FOX HUNT—$3,500 89.

Another fraud, which emptied the treasury of over three thousand dollars, to reward party favorites, was the act of pretending to employ an agent to look after the State lands as indicated in the following fraudulent allowances:

1854.	Feb. 24.	To C. J. Gox, for expenses as agent of the State, appointed by the Gov.,.	$147 31
"	May 12.	For services as lumber agent, July 1, 1843, to March 1, 1854,...	660 00
"	"	Expenses as such agent, from July, 1853, to March, 1854,.........	147 31

It is manifest that the Board allowed his *expenses* (147 31) *twice*.

But Mr. Fox's account runs on:

1854.	Sept 21.	O. C. Fall, employed by C. J. Fox, agent for State lands, 92 days, at $1 50 per day,.......	138 00
"	"	Expenses during same time,.....	95 87
"	"	C. J. Fox, for services as agent of the State to prevent tresspassing on the public lands, Feb. 29, to Sept 16, 1854,.........	558 00
"	"	C. J. Fox, for expenses incurred as agent for State, March 1, to Sept. 1, 1854,................	426 66
Amount of Mr. Fox's allowances,...........			$2,173 15
The amount of his collections from trespassers, as shown by same report, is only..........			29 00
Balance against the State,...............			$2,144 15
To be increased by amount paid to Mr. Furlong, for services,..............................			25 00
			2,169 15
To A. & E. Gould, as Attorneys in pretended cases, and interest,........................			1,331 74
Loss to the State,........................			3,500 89

A GRAND SWINDLE OF $300,000.

In 1838 the State loaned its credit to the Detroit and Pontiac Railroad to the amount of *one hundred thousand dollars*, and took ample mortgage security for the payment with the interest. In 1848 the Democratic State officers fixed up a compromise or settlement of the whole amount, by which the $100,000 ample mortgage security was surrendered by the State, and the sum of $32,000 only was received in full payment for the whole original debt, and interest for ten years, which had not been paid. Thus, the State lost the original $100,000 and $60,000 interest, less the $32,000 received on the settlement. The difference over the $32,000 went into the hands of Democratic officials and favorites. The whole amount, with compound interest to this date, would increase the money in the Treasury over $300,000!

The Hon. Moses Hawks, the Democratic editor of the Allegan *Record*, and still a leading Democrat in the northwestern part of the State, in the *Record* of February 15th, 1849, characterised this transaction as the work of "*about half a dozen old hackneyed broken-down politicians, as bankrupt in moral character as they are in political integrity: some of whom have often been foisted into office by the intrigues and profuse expenditures of the ill-gotten pelf of the ballance, whose knavery has rendered them the object of so much indignation, suspicion and contempt with the people.*"

THE QUID-PRO-QUO.—HOW THE "CHOICE PETS" PAID FOR THEIR ELECTION, AND SWINDLED THE STATE.—RICH DEMOCRATIC AUTHORITY.

This grand swindle of the Detroit and Pontiac Railroad affair, by the Democratic State officials, is made still more transparent by the further developments of Mr. Hawks. In the same number of the Allegan *Record*, quoted above, speaking of the system of frauds inaugurated by the Democratic State officials, Mr. Hawks further refers to this great swindle in the following emphatic language:

"The beauties of the system did not fully appear till the *choice pets* were installed into office, when, as the *quid pro quo* for *their election*, they (one in the Senate and one in the House) procured the passage of act after act, 'for the *relief* of the Detroit and Pontiac Railroad Company,' *by means of which*, the head *devil*, the Napoleon of scoundrels, finally succeeded in shaving the State out of the sum of $120,000."

It is pertinent to remark in this connection, that JOHN J. ADAM, now the Democratic candidate for Auditor General, was *then* Auditor General; and that GEO. B. COOPER, *now* the Democratic candidate for Congress in the first Congressional District, was *then* the Democratic State Treasurer, and that *both* of these Democratic candidates for election in 1858, were connected with the fraudulent compromise of the Detroit and Pontiac Railroad debt, by which the State was swindled as above shown. They are also among the "*half dozen old hackneyed broken-down politicians, as bankrupt in moral character as they are in political integrity,*" spoken of by the Hon. Moses Hawks, one of the strictest Democrats in the State.

Do the people of Michigan desire to see such men again foisted upon the State?

A SAMPLE CANDIDATE, WITH VOUCHERS.

The Democratic party have placed Edward Kanter in nomination for the important office of State Treasurer—an office requiring the highest order of business talents, as well as the most sterling and unwavering integrity. The following vouchers, paid by the Democratic State Auditor in 1853, show *two things;* first, the business capacity of the Democratic candidate for Treasurer; and, second, the dishonesty of the Democratic party officials in paying for the first translation when they knew it was not properly done:

STATE OF MICHIGAN,

1853. To Edward Kanter, Dr.

Jan'y. For translation of the Governor's Annual Message into the German Language,... $75 00

(Upon the above voucher is the following endorsement:)

"Allowed and paid at $50 00, Feb. 11, 1853."

Here follows another voucher for the same work, done over again, and paid for again, to another party, because the first translation was imperfect and worthless:

STATE OF MICHIGAN,
1853. To Dr. Rudolph, Dr.
Jan'y. For *re-translation* of Mr. Kanter's translation of the Governor's Annual Message, $40 00
Endorsed: "Allowed and paid Feb. 11, 1853."

Both these vouchers were audited and paid the same day, and of course it must have been known that one of them was a *fraud* upon the Treasury, though a favor to a political partizan. Do the people of the State desire to elect to office men engaged in such fraud and incompetency?

A SWINDLE OF $1,200—PROHIBITED BY THE CONSTITUTION.

The Constitution, chapter 4, section 22, expressly prohibits payment for "constructive" printing; but in the face of this plain provision of the constitution, the Democratic State officials of 1854—it has been found by examining the vouchers on file—paid a fraudulent claim for constructive printing—or, in other words, paid twice for the *same work*, as proved by the following vouchers:

STATE OF MICHIGAN, per Sec. of State,
1854. To GEO. W. PECK, DR.
Dec. 23. To printing Census Statistics, &c., 1854, composition 3,030,000 ems, at 33c,....$999 90
Endorsed "Allowed and paid Dec. 29, 1854."

Here follows another voucher which includes pay for exactly the *same work* at exactly the same price—there being only *one composition* for the same charges for printing:

STATE OF MICHIGAN, per State Ag. Soc.,
1854. To GEO. W. PECK, DR.
Dec. 23. To printing Report of Mich. State Agricultural Society, composition 4,858,770 ems, at 33c,....................$1,603 39
Endorsed Correct, and paid Dec. 29, 1854.

The amount of $999 90 was here allowed in the second voucher, after having been paid in the first—the Census certificates being included in the report of the State Agricultural Society—which with the interest to this time would have amounted to $1,280. This sum, which justly belongs to the Treasury, was fraudulently paid over to a political partisan, upon a false voucher, for *constructive* printing, expressly *prohibited* by the constitution!

GRAND THEFT OF **$155,708 57** FROM THE EDUCATIONAL FUND.

A careful examination of the official reports show that the most sacred of all our funds—those set apart for the education of the youth of Michigan—have not escaped from the thieving and plundering practices of former Democratic administrations.

UNIVERSITY FUND.

The interest and other items on account of University Fund received, but not *accounted* for, as shown by official record, are as follows:

1847,	Interest account,....................		$221 24
1848.	Penalty "		136 29
1849.	Interest "		186 54
1851.	Interest " $689 53		
"	Principal " 129 50		
			819 03
1852.	Principal account,............. 602 75		
"	Interest " 1,110 72		
			1,713 47
	Total small items in 5 years, to 1852,......		3,076 57

Original sales of University lands,............	612,519 14
Reduced by forfeiture and apprisal,..........	110,397 58
Actual sales,..........................	$503,121 56
The actual amount received on account of these sales of University lands, according to the reports of Commissioner of Land Office,........................	$271,771 84
Amount received by State Treasurer of the above as shown by his book,............	246,161 33
Amount stolen by Commissioner of Land Office,	**$25,610 51**

These amounts of fraud upon the University Fund have been discovered in a brief examination of the records and reports, and it is confidently believed that a more thorough examination would result in still more startling developments. We now come to the

PRIMARY SCHOOL FUND.

The peculations, frauds and pilferings from this sacred fund, seems to have been still more numerous than from the University fund. We add a brief statement of the condition of the fund at various times, showing the deficiencies:

Dec. 1, 1842. Receipts on account of *principal*,		$121,332 73
" " Amount loaned,....	$84,820 03	
" " Amount in Treasury,	30,533 59	
		115,353 59
Stole on account of principal,..........		$5,979 14

On account of Interest.

Received on account of interest,............		92,127 05
School moneys appropriated,......	$69,141 80	
Expenses,......................	10,502 74	
In hands of agents,..............	1,777 72	
Uncurrent funds,................	958 00	
		82,380 26
		9,746 79

The above deficiencies are reported in the report of Franklin Sawyer, Jr., Superintendent of Public Instruction for 1842. These are frauds up to 1842, but to exhibit the total losses in these funds down to the year 1854, when the Republican party assumed control of State affairs, we will show the aggregate of receipts and expenditures.

1.—The Principal.

Receipts, according to Report of Land Office,.		$737,721 84
Of which was loaned,...........	$84,820 00	
Expenses paid,................	13,587 40	
In Treasury, Nov. 30, 1857,......	630,742 94	
		729,150 34
Deficiency on account of principal,........		8.571 50

2.—The Interest.

Total receipts are given at................		$667,931 00
Expenditure,..................	$605,837 07	
In Treasury, Nov. 30, 1857,.......	36,430 78	
		642,267 85

Deficiency on interest account,............	25,663 15
On account of Principal, as above,..........	8,571 50
" Sales of Univ. lands, as above,..	25,610 51
Int. and Prin., in small items, as noted above,	3,076 57
Total Principal and Interest	62,921 73

Add "in hands of Agents," 1842,*	1,777 72
" Uncurrent funds, "	958 00
" worthless loans to individuals, sixteen years ago,†	11,900 00
	$77,557 45
Add compound interest on $30,602 13, of the above for 16 years,	62,785 38
Add compound interest on $46,955 32 for four years,	15,365 74
GRAND TOTAL,	**$155,708 57!!!**

GOVERNMENT STOCK BANK FRAUD—TOKENS OF DEMOCRATIC HONESTY.

The fraud by which the people of the State were swindled out of from $65,000 to $100,000 by the Government Stock Bank operation, is already familiar to the tax-payers who lost the amount. The facts are simply these: the Government Stock Bank, located at Ann Arbor, deposited public stocks with the State Treasurer to secure the redemption of its circulation. The stocks were used to redeem the circulating notes, when the State officers in 1854, instead of *canceling the notes and burning them*, as the law required, took them from the State Treasury vaults and *put them into circulation again*, on their own account and for their own private benefit. Of course there was no Stocks for their redemption, and the people who held the notes had to lose them. The swindlers themselves have boasted of their using $65,000, but the total amount of notes thus fraudulently put afloat is believed to be $100,000! and the people now hold this amount of Government Stock bills as tokens of Democratic honesty!

GRAND RECAPITTULATION—A BIRD'S EYE VIEW.

We will here recapitulate the frauds heretofore referred to, in order to give a bird's eye view of Democratic honesty and financeering in our State affairs. As will be seen in future pages, the amount dishonestly abstracted from the Treasury by Democratic officials previous to 1854, amounts to $319,733 70 *more than enough to pay off the State debt*, and would pay all expenses of State government at $100,000 a year, for over twenty-six years to come, or open a free school for every scholar in the State for an almost indefinite time, or build twenty magnificent colleges, or buy every poor man in the State a magnificent farm. The amount, with interest, is nearly *Three Million of Dollars!!*

First 10 years, loss in sale of Railroads,	$2,000,000 00
Amount of interest on balances, not paid over,	73,446 14
Fraudulent accounts allowed Dec., 1854,	60,000 00
Bill twice paid to Peck, and interest,	675 00
Fraudulent re-issue of Bonds in 1854, and interest,	3,000 00
Elwood & Co., Flat Cap fraud,	1,377 28
Cost of a Fox hunt,	3,500 89
Detroit and Pontiac Railroad swindle,	300,000 00
Paid Kanter for *not* translating Governor's message,	50 00
Constructive printing to Geo. W. Peck,	1 280 00
Grand theft from Educational funds,	155,708 57
Government Stock Bank Fraud,	100,000 00
Total amount due State Treasury from Democratic officials,	**$2,699,037 88**

WHAT THE REPUBLICANS HAVE DONE.

That the administration of State affairs, since the Republican party assumed control in 1855, have been eminently honest, wise and frugal, is a matter of pride with every member of the Republican party, as well as with every tax-payer in the State. Upon the question of finances and expenditures, we invite the most exacting scrutiny of the opponents of the administration—with the fullest knowledge that not one dollar has been *stolen* from the Treasury—as was so frequently practised under Democratic rule—and that every dollar has been properly accounted for, and the various disbursements made in accordance with acts of the Legislature and the provisions of law.

The various reckless charges made by the Democratic organs, are of the most groundless character, and only prove the desperation to which they are reduced in the impudent attempt to be restored to power, after having PLUNDERED the State of nearly THREE MILLIONS OF DOLLARS, before they were ousted in 1854. It now remains for the tax-payers of the State to say whether the former practice of robbery and plunder of the State Treasury shall be re-installed by restoring the Democratic party to power and office; or whether the affairs of the State shall be continued in the hands of the Republican party whose nominees are known to be men of purity of character and integrity of purpose.

WHAT BECAME OF $83,962 71.

When the Democratic party surrendered power in 1854, the last report of the State Treasurer showed $553,004 08 in the Treasury, which report was *false*—the real amount being only $469,041 37. The discrepancy of $83,962 71 being spent and paid out during the month of December, 1854, in paying the fraudulent allowances to Gilbert & Co., Phœnix Bank, Job Brookfield, Geo. W. Peck, A. Gould, Elwood & Co., Bronson Knight & Ingalls, &c., which amounts and transactions are referred to in previous pages. As there is nothing to conceal with regard to the financial affairs of the State under the Republican party, we present a concise statement of them from official sources,—allowing $83,962 71 of fraudulent payments by Democrats in December, 1854, to stand, as reported, in the hands of the Republican Treasurer:

---

*The Report of 1842 reports "in hands of agents," the sum of $1,777 72, which appears to have been in the hands of one *Beeson*, for the recovery of which a suit was commenced; but we find no account of the suit having been terminated, or the money received:—so we place the amount to the loss of the fund.

† These loans, amounting to $11,900, as shown by the records, were made mostly to political partisans and favorites, without any adequate security being exacted for the payment, and apparently without any expectation that it would ever be returned to the Treasury. In fact, it appears to have been disbursed with the dishonest intention of defrauding the Treasury to reward political favorites.

Comparison of the Raceipts and Disbursements for the fiscal years 1855, 1856 *and* 1857.

The amount in the Treasury at the close of the fiscal year ending Nov. 30, 1854, was..	$553,004 08
Receipts during the fiscal year 1855,........	588,396 93
Total,..............................	1,141,401 01
Disbursements for same period,..........	624,777 88
Leaving on hand at the close of the fiscal year 1855, and at the commencement of 1856,..	516,623 13
Amount received durisg the fiscal year of 1856, was............................	511,271 70
Total,..............................	1,027,894 83
Disbursements for same period,...........	639,879 06
Leaving on hand at the close of the fiscal year of 1856, and at the commencemeni of 1857,	388,015 77
Receipts for fiscal year 1857,..............	450,653 85
Total,..............................	838,669 62
Disbursements for same period,...........	679,979 19
Leaving on hand at close of fiscal year 1857, and commencement of the next,........	$158,699 43

The surplus, it will be seen was thus reduced as follows:

1855,......................................	$ 36,380 95
1856,......................................	128,607 36
1857,......................................	229,325 34
Total,..............................	394,313 65

WHAT WAS DONE WITH THE MONEY.

The Democratic presses have raised a blind and insane howl about the expenditures of the moneys that have come into the State Treasury since 1854, which induces us to show the legitimate and proper uses to which they have been applied. There has been paid during the three years, of state debts, in part, which were made by the Democratic party many years ago, and for other purposes, as follows:

State debts, made by Democrats,............	$160 305 02
Expen es of two Legislatures,..............	43,111 52
State Prison, repairs and additions,.........	69,624 37
House of Correction for juveniles,...........	43,770 46
Awards of State Auditors,...................	119-706 03
Interest on Trust Funds,....................	428 301 74
Expenses of Judiciary,......................	47,145 46
Salaries of State officers,..................	42,920 24
Publishing laws and Legislative printing,.....	11,241 77
Asylums, (Deaf and Dumb and Insane,).....	161.579 96
Agricultural College,.......................	93.159 46
Moneys paid to counties,...................	252,938 78
State Pri on expense,.......................	59,000 00
Interest on State debts made by Democrats,..	271.929 70

Aside from these, there are numerous smaller disbursements, as provided by the constitution and the laws, such, as on account of the State Agricultural Society, Fugitives from Justice, Stste Library, Coroners' Fees, Teachers' Institutes, Specific Taxes refunded to Upper Peninsular, Wolf Bounties, Military, Journal of Education, Postage, Normal School, &c., &c.

THE BENEFICENT PUBLIC WORKS.

By the foregoing table it will be seen that large appropriations have been made to complete the Asylums, which were commenced by the Democratic party, and upon which they expended about $2,000 in 1853 and $25,631 54 in 1854, as appears by the last reports of Auditor General Swegles. The people have listened to a large amount of insane groans of the Democratic leaders and journals, about the appropriations to complete these buildings; but these groans—mere scare crows to frighten—do not avail much in the way of political capital among the people who acknowledge the wisdom and necessity of these Beneficent Institutions, and are willing to appropriate the requisite amount of money for the purpose of endowing them. In fact, the people of Michigan, in framing the Constitution under Democratic auspices, provided for these Institutions, and they feel proud of their ability to pattern after all Civilized and Christian States in providing Deaf, Dumb, Blind and Insane Asylums for the comfort and relief of those who have been deprived of their natural faculties for the enjoyment of the various blessings of life and liberty guaranteed by our Republican form of Government. It would seem that none but those bereft of reason, or deaf to all the impulses of humanity and the influences of the Christian religion, would ever interpose objections to just appropriations for such noble purposes; yet we find the moral and mental happiness—the improvement and restoration, the misery and misfortune of these classes of individuals thrown into the scale with political capital for the Democratic party. Thus all the benevolent attempts of Michigan to follow the example of her sister States, in providing Asylums for the unfortunate, are sought to be crushed out by vile detraction and falsehoods, merely that the plundering, pilfering Shylocks of the Democratic party may regain access to the vaults of the State Treasury, and again practice their frauds upon the peoples' money, to enrich themselves. The enormous sum of *over Two and a Half Million of Dollars* which should be in the Treasury, but which has been pilfered away by Democratic officials—as shown in former pages—ought to be a convincing argument to them that having been caught in the mal-administration of public affairs, the people do not again require their services in the same way—at least not until the Beneficent Public Works and Asylums of the State are finished, and the old State State debt, created by the Democrats, is paid off, by a few years of prudent and honest administration of affairs by the Republican party.

OTHER APPROPRIATIONS.

Besides the appropriations to the Asylums. it will be discovered that the Republicans have taken up a large amount of the State debt contracted by the Democratic party in years past.. They have also paid a large amount of *Interest* on the State debt, which would have been extinguished long ago had all the money fraudulently taken from the Treasury been applied by the Democratic party to that object. Nearly half a million of dollars, in interest, has been paid by the Republican administration on the "Trust Funds" alone, which the Democratic party *borrowed to carry on the government*, and to exhibit a full Treasury and furnish a larger pile to pilfer from—perhaps upon the principle that small slices from a large loaf would not be so easily missed!

The cost of enlargement of the State Prison, facilities to meet the wants of the State, in providing for criminals, has been largely increased in re-building portions built under the management of Democratic agents, and found to be entirely worthless. The expenses for the salary of State officers and the expenses of the judiciary are regulated by the Constitution and the acts of of Democratic Legislatures. The endowment of an Agricultural College for the education of the farmers' sons of Michigan in the enoblidg pursuits of agriculture and tilling of the soil, is an endowment that will reflect honor and credit upon the State of Michigan, whose pioneer example has already been followed by several of her sister States, much older in the confederacy. This being a pioneer enterprise by this State, the Democratic journals, for political capital, have made it a point to offer up hideous forebodings of the result, with no untried effort to render it odious and unpopular, by falsehood and misrepresentation,—yet the far more numerous applications than the present limited facilities of the College will accommodate, *by the farmers from all parts of the State*, for the education of their sons at their own peculiar Institution, sufficiently demonstrates that the Agricultural College meets with the confidence and hearty approval of the great agricultural interests of the whole State, without regard to, and above all merely party or political considerations.

The awards of the Board of State Auditors have been published in detail in the annual reports, and will bear the test of the most riged investigation for integrity and legality. On the subject of expenditures, the State Central Committee refer with the utmost pride and confidence, that they have been properly made by the representatives of the Republican party.

DECREASED RECEIPTS.

The great source of revenue to swell the receipts in 1854, the last year of Democratic rule, was the sale of public lands, which, owing to immigration setting in another direction, has been falling off ever since.

Receipts, 1854.,	$610,699 97	
" 1854,	588.396 93	
Diminution for 1855,		$22,303 04
Receipts, 1856,	511,271 70	
Diminution for 1856,		77,125 23
Receipts, 1857,	450,653 85	
Diminution, 1857,		60,617 85
Decrease in three years,		160,046 12

Comparative Table of the Sale of Primary School, Unerversily, Normal School and Asylum Lands, for 1854, 1855, 1856 *and* 1857.

Amount sold in 1854,	$409,675 73	
" " 1855,	159,648 89	
Decrease in 1855,		$250,026 84
Amount sold in 1855,	159,648 89	
" " 1856,	110,671 98	
Decrease in 1856,		48,976 91
Amount sold in 1856,	110,671 98	
" " 1857,	50,254 55	
Decrease in 1857,		60,,417 42
Making the total aggregate decrease of sales as compared,		359,421 18

The sales of these lands for 1854 exceed the combined amounts of 1855, 1856 and 1857, in the sum of $89,100 31.

Notwithstanding this decrease in the receipts of the Treasury, the Republican administration has promptly met the State indebtedness as it fell due, also the interest on old *Democratic State debts*, and thus protected the faith and credit of the State; and also made the necessarily large expenditures for the various Asylums. The credit of the State was *never so good* as at present, in the market where the bonds are held, being quoted higher, comparatively, than those of any other State in the Union.

WHERE THEY GOT MONEY TO SPECULATE WITH.

The Democratic leaders boast that they left towards a half a million surplus in the Treasury. It will be well to look, and see where they got the money—whether by frugal aud prudent management of affairs, or by borrowing it, and paying interest upon it.

In his Annual Report for 1852, the Auditor General Reports that the Democratic party had borrowed a large amount to carry on the government, and stated in his Report that "the amount due the Educational Funds are considered permanent loans, and will so remain." They thus commenced a system of appropriating these Funds by law, which would have been well enough, had they not involved the State for the *Interest*, while the officials used the amount for private speculations *without* returning any interest to the State for the use of it. The indebtedness to the Trust Funds increased as follows:

1852, due Trust Funds,		$263,080 53
1853, " "		466,956 26
1854, " "		660,174 74

Thus it will be seen how rapidly the Democrats accumulated funds, and where they got them from—and how so large a surplus in the Treasury. The fraud upon the Treasury amounted to over $70,000! which went into the pockets of individual speculators! For these large amounts of money in their hands, for several years up to 1854, they paid into the Treasury only the insignificant sum of $1,553 86! whereas the Republicans, in only three years time, for the unexpended balances of money on hand, have paid into the Treasury the sum of SIXTY-ONE THOUSAND FOUR HUNDRRD AND EIGHTY-FOUR DOLLARS AND FIFTY-FIVE CENTS, being at the rate of 17 per cent, while the Democrats paid at the rate of less than *one-fourth per cent!* Had the Democrats paid interest for the money they had, at the same per cent, it would have added more than SEVENTY-THREE THOUSAND DOLLARS to the Treasury. The Democratic officials used the surplus funds for private speculations,—loaning them out at from 5 to 8 per cent, and pocketed the amount, while the Republicans have procured the highest rate of interest possible where the funds were deposited, and placed the amount in the Treasury where it properly belongs. This is a fair sample of the honesty with which the two parties have managed the affairs of the State for the interest of the tax payers.

The people have now an opportunity at the ballot boxes, to choose between the two. If they want the old system of peculations, fraud and pilfering of the public funds, and all kinds of dishonest management in State affairs, they will restore the Democratic party to power; if they want the affairs of the State prudently and honestly managed, as they have been since 1854, they will elect the Republican ticket.

ABOUT THE STATE DEBT!!

It is an interesting fact, to the pockets of tax-payers, to see how the State debt has been managed by the Republican and by the Democratic party. A brief statement of the subject will place it before the public in a light that must be convincing to the people as to which party had better have the management of State affairs. In the Annual Report of John J. Adam, Auditor General, for 1849, he reports the State debt, exclusive of assets, at $2,071,962 90. From this time onward, until 1854, the State debt increared, as well as the debt to the Trust Funds, as we have already shown. Thus, exclusive of due to Trust Funds:

Report of J. J. Adam, 1849, $1,795,520 46
" J. Swegles, Jr., 1853, 2,339,392 07
" J. Swegles, Jr., 1854, 2,531,545 70

There is no account in the disbursement of money for these years, of any for the payment of much of the of interest upon the State indebtedness, although the party leaders and presses always pretended to the people that they were promptly paying the interest. It appears from this that they never paid interest, but allowed it to accumulate and increase the debt, while they were boasting of the large amount of funds in the Treasury! We appeal to the tax-payers to say if this was wise policy. While they were paying interest on the money on hand, they were using it for private speculations and cheating the State out of the Interest!

THE STATE DEBT THEN AND NOW.

According to the Report of John Swegles, Jr., Auditor General, 1854, and the Report of the present Republican State Treasurer, and also the Auditor General, the State debt for the two periods was as follows:

Democratic Report, 1854, $2,531,545 70
Republican do 1857, 2,269,467 48

Less now than in 1854, $262,078 22

Besides the amount that the original debt has been reduced, the Republicans have paid about $272,000 00 *Interest* on the public debt as it became due, besides meeting all the other requirements of the State, including the large sums for the building of the Asylums. This, with a largely decreased revenue, as shown in a former article, will be sufficient proof that nothing has been squandered, but all expenditures have been wisely and judiciously expended. During the year 1858, $97,000 of the bonds issued to the Detroit and Pontiac Railroad in 1838, for which the security was afserwards fraudulently given up, has fallen due, besides $99,000 00 of University Bonds, all of which have been satisfactorily provided for without increasing the State indebtedness a single dollar.

RATE OF TAXATION UNDER DEMOCRATIC AND REPUBLICAN ADMINISTRATIONS—100 PER CENT IN FAVOR OF REPUBLICANS!

The question of taxation is one which appeals immediately to the pockets of the people. The amount of taxes levied to carry on the government, by any party in power, for a series of years, is a good indication of the honesty and frugality of the administration. With this view of comparing taxation by the late and present admiuistration, we subjoin the following official table, covering a period of ten years:

DEMOCRATIC.

Year.	Valuation.	Tax.	per cent in mills.
1848,..........	$29,908,769 00	$150,716 99	5.04
1849,..........	28,999,202 00	102,404 00	3.53
1850,..........	29,384,270 00	113,768 00	3.87
1851,..........	30,976,270 00	106,000 00	3.42
1852,..........	30,976,270 00	110 000 00	3.55
1853,..........	120,362,474 00	10,000 00	0.08
1854,..........	120,362,474 00	30,000 00	0.25
Total,....	390,969,729 00	622,892 00	1.59
REPUBLICAN.			
1855,..........	120,362,474 00	40,000 00	0.33
1856,..........	137,663,009 00	65,000 00	0.47
1857,..........	137,663,009 00	85,065 00	0 61
Total,....	395,688,492 00	190,065 00	0.47

For 7 years under Democratic rule, average State tax per year, ...$88 984 00
Average rate per cent, or mills per dollar, 1½ mills!
For the period of three years under Republican rule, average State tax per year. only.............$63,335 00
Average rate per cent, or mills per dollar, only 47-100 of a mill!!
Total valuation, 7 years Democratic,.....$390;969,929 00
" " 3 years Republican,..... 395,688,492 00
Total tax, 7 years Democratic,.$622,892 00
" " 3 years Republican,. 190,065 00

These figures are deemed a complete answer to all the charges by the Democrats of exhorbitant taxation by the Republicans. These figures show that the average annual tax by the Republicans, since they have been in power, has been $25,629 less than during the seven years of preceding rule by the Democrats, when they had the benefit of very large receipts from the sale of public lands, amounting to $90,000 more in the single year 1854, from this source. than from the same source for the whole three years of 1855–6 and 7. The rate of taxation for three years of Republican rule—and that upon a valuation of over $96,000,000 greater—has been a difference of *more than one hundred per cent* in favor of the Republicans, as compared with previous years! The Democrats may point to a low rate of tax for the last two years of their rule. This is readily explained. They omitted to levy some $40,000 these two years, for Asylum purposes, as the law *expressly commanded* them to do. This was the way they made a show of light taxes for two years. The average rate of tax by the Democrats for seven years was 1.59 or over one and a half mills upon the dollar. The average by Republicans has been 47-100 of a mill upon the dollar. The difference in 47 cents, and one dollar and 59 cents, shows the difference in taxation under Democratic and Republican administrations.

ANOTHER VIEW OF TAXES.

The Democratic presses attempt to charge the onerous aggregate taxes in certain localities upon the State administration, whereas the fault, if there is any, is with counties and towns and cities. To show what proportion of the tax paid, is for State purposes, we will take for a sample, the county of Wayne, which is intensely Democratic in its local administration.

1857. Total county tax,	$76,964 67
1857. Total State tax,	11,832 30

The county tax is about *seven* times greater than the State tax. But we will take the city of Detroit for a brighter example of Democratic taxation, as compared with the Republican State administration. Allow that the city pays one-half of the State and County tax, which is comparatively not far from the fact, and the taxes show as follows for the city for 1857:

County tax for the city,	$38,482 33
State " " "	5,916 15
City "	112,072 43
Sewer "	4,651 00
School "	38,345 35
Road "	12,701 95
Paving "	50,000 00
Side walk tax,	5,000 00
	267,169 21

This is a ratio of less than one to 45 of State tax—or in other words, while the Republican State administration call upon the tax-payers of Detroit to pay ONE DOLLAR in taxes, the *Democratic* government of the county of Wayne and of the city of Detroit, call upon them for FORTY-FIVE DOLLARS!! The Democratic journals and politicians would have the people believe that the State Republican administration is to be held responsible for all these taxes, while in fact it has nothing to do with only one dollar in 45 of it!

A similar comparison, by the *Lansing State Republican*, of the county of Ingham, where there is no large city tax, shows that the sixteen men in the county who are assessed the highest—while they pay a total of $715 79 in taxes, only the insignificant sum of $27 80 of the above is State tax! leaving $687 99 of the amount paid for local purposes, with which the State administration has nothing to do. The result is about the same in all the counties.

SPECIFIC TAXES.

The opponents of the Republican party have sought to convey the impression that the specific taxes collected, which are increasing each year, should have a tendency to lessen direct taxes levied for the support of the State government. This impression, like others sought to be created against the Republican party, is either founded upon ignorance, or is the result of premeditated dishonesty by those who attempt to convey such falsehoods.

Article 14, section 1, of the Constitution, enacted by the Democratic party, enacts that "*all specific taxes*, except those for mining companies of the Upper Peninsula, shall be applied in paying the interest upon the primary school, university, and other educational funds, and interest and principal of the State debt," &c., &c. The specific taxes from the mining companies are paid back to the counties in the Upper Peninsula for local improvements; as provided by law. The specific taxes, therefore, cannot be applied to carrying on the government, and that Democratic thunder is effectually silenced by the Constitution, as quoted above.

INCREASE OF BUSINESS AND EXPENSES.

The great bulk of State expenses connected with the departments, arises from the return and collection of taxes, and the expenses increase in ratio with the business. In order to show the extravagance of the Democratic administration of affairs, and the economy of the Republican administration, a comparison of business for three years under each is submitted.

Amount of Unpaid Taxes returned.

1852, Democratic,	$140,549 89
1853, "	113,965 43
1854, "	128,977 36
	383,492 68
1855, Republican,	150,681 55
1856, "	189,261 05
1857, "	265,044 00
	604,986 60

Here it will be observed the business has very nearly doubled in three years under the Republican administration.

Its bearing on the Ice question.

The Democratic journals and politicians have been seized with an agonizing *cold sweat* on the subject of $25,97 for ice for the offices in 1857. To show, according to their own logic, that the Democrats actually swindled the State out of nearly $30 for ice in 1854, we submit a comparative statement:

Democrats—Ice in 1854,	$41 53
Republicans—Ice in 1857,	25 97
	15 56

Here is $15 56 in favor of the Republicans, with double the amount of business, and consequently requiring double the number of men to do it. From this showing, it should have required only half the amount of ice in 1854 to have done half the amount of business that was done in 1857—consequently the amount of ice proper for 1854 would have been only $12 98, which would be in proportion to the quantity used by the Republicans in 1857. This shows that the Democratic State officers in 1854 swindled the State ont of just $29 00 for ice, which they charged for but did not use.

A BOGUS COIN DETECTED.

The Democratic Treasury suckers have put forth and are extensively circulating a four page pamphlet signed "*Jefferson*," and purporting to be written by a "Republican" who voted for Fremont. It will be quite sufficient, to stamp this base coinage as bogus, to say that it was written by *Samuel N. Gantt*, an avowed Democrat of the Douglas, Dred Scott, Slavery extending persuasion. This "Republican," *alias* "Jefferson," was elected a Democratic Justice in Pontiac in 1838—went to Detroit and was elected a Justice in 1841; and was removed by Governor Barry for *gross malfeasance in office*, on the 21st June, 1842, upon charges which appear at full length upon file in the State department. He was subsequently distinguished in connection with extraordinary bills for stationery, poaket knives, &c., for the Legislature in Detroit.

THE CHARACTER OF ANOTHER DOCUMENT.

Those who would be returned, as plunderers, to the State Treasury, have issued another document, called "Facts for the tax-payers and voters of Michigan," which is only a tissue of gross misrepresentations, falsehoods and unfounded charges against the Republican administration. This document being thrown broadcast over the State is signed by the Democratic State Central Committee, headed by the name of *Michael Shoemaker*, a tool of James Buchanan, and drawing thousands upon thousands of dollars from the people's money each year, as Collector of the Port of Detroit. He is the man who, in paying off a deputy in his office, retained $10, on a voucher of $40, which he sent to Washington as the expenses of his office! Whether the 25 per cent thus retained from the wages of employees is for the purpose of issuing the above noticed false political document, or for private gain, or for the purpose of corrupting the ballot boxes at the approaching election, and endorsing the pro-slavery policy of James Buchanan, we shall leave for the public to judge.

Another name, upon whose authority the above mentioned veracious and *valuablo* document is issued, is that of *S. Dow Elwood*, who made out a false voucher for $1,076, for 315 reams flat cap paper, in 1854, and got it allowed and paid by a dishonest Board of Democratic State Auditors, who knew the paper had never been furnished, and that the thing was a downright *swindle* from beginning to end. Mr. *S. Dow Elwood* has since admitted the fraud. This is the kind of authority upon which electioneering Democratic documents are circulated, making charges against the integrity of the Republican administration!! Will the people, or "tax-payers and voters of Michigan," heed the falsehoods issuing from such sources, when no proofs beyond their bare assertions are offered to sustain their charges? Another document to the people, purporting to be "issues before them," and issued by order of the same "State Central Committee," from the *Jacksonian* print, at Pontiac, is another budget of fabrications, entitled to the same credit as the above mentioned and no more. Any other similar document that may appear against the Republicans, previous to election day, will be of the like character, and unworthy of belief or consideration.

THE HAND SLED AND WHEELBARROW QUESTION.

The Democratic journals have charged extravagance and attempted to make themselves jolly over the fact that the Republican State officers purchased a hand sled at $7, for the economy and convenience of conveying documents and materials from and to the State Capitol, fire-proof offices, &c., &c. That the premeditated dishonesty of those making such charges may be seen, we compare similar accouts in 1854 with those of 1857:

1854.		
Feby. 24.	Wheelbarrow,......................	$1 12
May 12.	To Hobbs for Wheelbarrow,........	1 25
" "	" " "	9 00
Nov. 30.	To Newson for Hand Cart,..........	17 00
Total for 1854, (Democratic,).................		28 37
Total for 1857, (Republican,).................		7 00
In favor of Republicans,......................		21 37.

THE COST OF A DEMOCRATIC WELL.

In the accounts audited in 1854 are the following, showing the cost of a Democratic well.

Feb. 24.	Digging well, (30 foot,)..................	$80 45
	Stone and hauling,......................	14 00
May 12.	To Samuel Cooper, for repairing well,....	6 00
Nov. 30.	To S. Cooper, for taking up and relaying well, and furnishing stone, 30 feet,.....	67 50
		167 95

The current price in this part of the State, for digging and stoning up a well is one dollar per foot for the first twenty feet, and one dollar and twenty-five cents per foot for the next ten feet. The well actually cost only $32 50 according to ordinary prices, leaving a surplus of $135 45 as the amount plundered out of the State.

A PUMPING ADMINISTRATION.

The *peculiar* facilities of the retiring administration of 1854, for fraudulently pumping money from the Treasury under color of law—(see Job Brookfield, Phœnix Bank, Peck, Elwood & Co., and other transactions)—has already been shown. It is therefore supposed that the following items for pumps during a single year, was only the introduction of a new system of suction from the Treasury vaults;

1854.			
Feb. 24.	B. B. & W. R Noyes, for pumps,	....	$16 93
May 12.	McKibbin & Co.,	"	28 48
	"Hobbs,"	"	75
	H. Angel,	"	2 50
	O. B. Rice,	"	6 16
Nov 30.	M H. Webster,	"	105 00
	H. Angel,	"	3 50
	Total for Democratic pumps, 1854,	....	163 32

Whether the amount for pumps for each year previous, under Democratic rule, was much larger than for 1854, or whether it was a trifle less for some of the years, we have not the time to go into a thorough examination of the items to see. One thing is very certain. This large number of *pumps* were not among the *assets* of the retiring Democratic party. The Republican officials have never been able to find them. Whethey they were for the private use of political friends and favorites, outside of the circle of State officials, or whether the amounts were fictitious charges as another mode of pumping money from the Treasury vaults into the pockets of officials, is a question clouded in the utmost conjecture.

A SPIRITUAL ADMINISTRATION.

During the year 1854 there is a large number of blind items audited, as supplied to "State officers," designated "*sundries*," which is the only indication of their character, excepting the business of the persons to whom the accounts were audited. Some bills amounting to about one hundred dollars, were furnished by Wm. Hinman, then a *dealer in Spiritous Liquors!* We leave it for the public to judge of this transaction.

RATHER EXPENSIVE CHAIRS.

As a sample of the pretended cost of transporting five chairs from Detroit to Lansing, and their entire expense, we make the following extracts from the audited accounts for 1854:

Feb. 24.	Expense of Swegles to Detroit, to buy furniture,	$15 00
	Bill for 5 office chairs, J. W. Tillman,....	101 50
May 12.	To John Whiteley, for transportation of furniture from Detroit,..............	90 27
		206 77

Something over *eighteen dollars* a piece for the transportation of five office chairs, weighing perhaps 50 pounds each, from Detroit to Lansing, besides paying for them, looks *rather* extravagant, and should silence Democratic charges of extravagance against the Republican party.

THE GOLD PEN AND SUPER-ROYAL QUESTION.

The Treasury eaters, in their despair to regain access to the Treasury, have charged the Republican party with extravagance in the purchase of pens and super-royal paper. The accounts for these items under Democratic and Republican rule, compare as follows:

1854—Democratic,..........................	$5,679 18
1857—Republican, ...	4,176 91
In favor of Republicans,................	1,502 27

The same quality of super-royal paper audited to the Democrats in 1854 at *twenty-eight dollars* per ream, the Republicans procured for *twenty-six dollars*. This is only another proof of the frugality of the Republican administration. A careful examination of all the charges of extravagance against the Republican administration, result in the discovery that they are utterly false and unfounded, showing comparatively a large saving by them in the ordinary expenses of the State.

TRAVELING EXPENSES AND OTHER ITEMS.

We only refer to this charge of extravagance, as we have to others, to show the dishonesty of those making it. To show the thing in a proper light we place items of expenses for the same things, for 1854 and 1857, in juxtaposition, and leave it with the tax-payers to judge how much foundation there is for the charges:

	1854. Democratic.	1857. Republican.
Auditor General,................	$ 122 90	$ 77 65
Secretary of State,..............	186 50	225 00
Treasurer and deputy,..........	179 74	101 00
Com. of Land Office,............	1,106 89	240 00
Supt. Public Instruction,........	547 21	50 00
	2 143 24	693 65
		2,143 24
In favor of Repeblicans,....................		1,449 59

Again we compare:

1854.	Extra clerk hire, and extra att'y fees,...	$6,448 78
1857.	By Republicans, for same items,.......	2,775 38
		3,663 40

TESTIMONY ENOUGH.

We might extend this showing, with the same results, through the entire range of expenses by the two administrations—but the foregoing proof of positive dishonesty and fraud, to the amount of nearly *three millions of dollars*, as specified, besides a thousand smaller matters not included in the Grand Recapitulation, is evidence enough of the character of the preceding and the present administrations. We might go on and show from the record that just before the Treasury plunderers left in 1854, they allowed over $750 00 to two deputies in the departments—to one for 195, and the other for 196 "extra" days' work, making 391 "extra" days allowed to two persons!!—but would that be any plainer proof of fraud than has already been given? We think not, and therefore will not follow the subject any further, but leave it with the tax-payers at the ballot boxes in November.

A CHALLENGE TO FACE THE MUSIC.—A DEMOCRATIC WITNESS.

The Democrats having made a woeful howl about the expenditures for items in the departments, under the Republican administration, and paraded long lists of figures about gold-pens, pencils, super royal, flat-cap, letter, foolscap and wrapping paper, and other necessary articles, we challenge them to call a Democratic witness upon the stand, who is possessed of *personal knowledge* on all these subjects. From the 28th of February, 1855, to Sept. 3d, 1858, Mr. CHAS. W. BUTLER, a Democrat of the strictest sect, acted as Deputy Auditor General for Col. Whitney Jones, the Auditor, and with a full knowledge of the wants of the department, he made out, during that time, the orders for supplies, and is perfectly familiar with and fully cognizant of the *whole subject.* He knows what artictes have been bought and paid for. He knows whether an extravagant price has been paid. He knows whether any frauds have been practiced upon the treasury in the payment of these bills. Mr. Butler had special instructions to show all vouchers called for by Democratic wonder-seekers, and to answer all questions touching expenditures, &c., &c. The editors of the Lansing *State Journal* (Democratic), and the Democratic politicians, have been invited to free access, through Mr. *Butler*, of their own party, to the whole file of vouchers and facts connected with the Republican administration since 1854, to discover whatever they could, *if there existed* any wrong. *They have done so*, and fail to disclose a single dishonest transaction!

Mr. Butler, on leaving the office of Deputy Auditor General, on the 30th September past, was fully endorsed by the Lansing *State Journal* as a *sound and honest Democrat.* We challenge the *accusers of the Republican administration to call* Mr. CHARLES W. BUTLER *upon the witness' stand*, to give his testimony for or against the integrity of the Republican administration upon all these subjects of which he has *personal knowledge.* Let the accusers of the Republican party *face the music.*

The National Finances.

In connection with the former Democratic extravagance of our State administration, it is well to look to the unparalleled extravagance of the present *National* administration; as the result of the approaching State election will be claimed as an endorsement or condemnation of the profligate waste of money by James Buchanan. To exhibit this wastefulness to the easy comprehension of the people, we contrast it with former history.

It is startling to look at the increase in the expenditures of the Government, and the contrast between "economical Democracy" and the party charged with the profusion and wasteful disbursement:

Monroe's Administration, (four years,)		46,432,382 75
Adams' "		51,671,933 99
Jackson's " (second term,)		184,051,735 81
Van Buren's "		110,678,427 81
Harrison's "		78,163,312 81
Polk's "		165 481,013 33
Taylor's "	1st year, 29,724,261 92	
(Fillmore,)	2d yoar, 39,623,795 00	158,161,528 71
Pierce's Administration,		282,820,622 35

Now to show what James Buchanan spent in the past year of his extravagant and corrupt administration, we submit a statement of the money in the Treasury, left by Pierce when he retired, and what has come into his hands since, from the natural revenues of the customs, public lands, appropriations by Congress, public loans, &c.

Received from Pierce,	26,000,000 00
" " Revenues,	64,000,000 00
" " Treasury Notes,	20,000,000 00
" " Loan,	20,000,000 00
Total received by Buchanan,	130,000,000 00
Asked for and not granted by Congress...	8,000,000 00
	138,000,000 00

The Money all Gone.

By the issue of twenty millions of treasury notes, and the twenty million loan by the last Congress, the permanent national debt was *increased* forty millions of dollars in the first year of Buchanan's administration. The vast sum of *one hundred and thirty million* of dollars, placed in the hands of the President, as shown above, was all expended, and he asked for the appropriation of eight millions more, which Congress *refused to grant.* But this amount has been spent, and will come in in the appropriation for the next year as "deficiences"—making an aggregate of *one hundred and thirty-eight million of dollars in one year.* At this ratio, for the four years which Mr. Buchanan is saddled upon the nation, his expenses for the term will be FIVE HUNDRED AND FIFTY-TWO MILLION OF DOLLARS, or over *three hundred and nineteen millions* more than the expense of the weak and corrupt administration of Frankliu Pierce!

HOW THE MONEY WAS SPENT — WILL THE FREEMEN OF MICHIGAN ENDORSE IT?

When we consider that the United States is at peace with all the world, with no unusual demands for expenditures to carry on the government, it will be folly in the partizans of the national administration to attempt to vindicate it against the charge of gross corruption in squandering the public funds. No such attempt is made by any intelligent citizen who is well informed in the facts. It is a painful duty to state the purposes for which the great majority of the money has been applied. A due regard for our national reputation before the civilized world would snppress the statement; but as we deny that the heart of the nation responds to these acts of a corrupt party, it is a duty we owe to mankind to make a clean breast of it and state the truth. *The money has been spent in an unholy attempt to rivit* THE CHAINS OF HUMAN SLAVERY *upon the* FREE PEOPLE OF KANSAS, *and to extend the cursed institution of Slavery over more free territory!!* As humiliating as the statement may be to every patriot and lover of his country and her glorious fame, it is the truth; and one of the leading issues before the people of Michigan at *this election*, is the *endorsement*, or the *indignant condemnation* of this atrocious and wicked conduct of James Buchanan and the party that sustains his administration.

Will the people of Michigan endorse the extravagant, wasteful and corrupt squandering of one hundred and thirty-eight millions of dollars to extend slavery, by voting for the nominees of the Democratic party, or will they place their seal of condemnation upon their acts by voting for the Republican candidates?

DEMOCRATIC TABLE FOR REDUCING THE NATIONAL TREASURY, FOR THE BENEFIT OF SLAVERY, BY JAMES BUCHANAN.

It spends—

$138,000,000 a year!
11,500,000 a month!
2,654,000 a week!
377,000 a day!
15,708 an hour!
261 a minute!
4 35 a second!

We would simply ask, whether the tax-payers of Michigan wish to endorse and continue the expenditure of the public funds for *such purposes*, by voting for the Democratic ticket at the approaching election?

Rate for each Inhabitant.

Under the administration of Gen. Harrison in 1841, and under that of Taylor and Fillmore in 1850, the ratio of national expenses in the United States, was only *one dollar and twenty-two cents* per head to each inhabitant. Under the *slavery extending* administration of James Buchanan, the head and leader of the Democratic party, the average of national expenses for each individual is about FIVE DOLLARS AND FIFTY CENTS each!!

Who pays the cost?

As about three-quarters or more of the expenses of the Government are paid by the free Northern States, it can be very easily seen that the free laborers of the North are thus made te pay enormous amounts each year, to protect and extend the institution of human slavery, which is the leading policy of that party. Are the people of Michigan anxious to vote this large expenditure for slavery, by voting for the slavery-extending Democratic party? Let them answer in emphatic terms at the ballot box.

THE REAL ISSUE.

SLAVERY IN KANSAS—DEMOCRATIC POLICY.

The story of Kansas can be told in a brief space. The *policy* of the Democratic party is to extend the dominion of human slavery over the free territories of the United States. It requires no argument to prove this proposition. The history of Democratic party tactics for half a century is living proof. In 1820 a compact between slavery and freedom was formed and ratified, by which slavery was never to march its bloody track across the line of 36 deg. 30 min. By the "Missouri Compromise," all the territory north of that line was dedicaten th freedom *forever*, without a contest with slavery. But in 1854, the demand of the slave-breeders of the South became rampant for more dominion. Slavery fixed its grasping eyes upon the *free* territory of KANSAS, as a victim to be despoiled of its beauty and its freedom. To accomplish this, the South demanded the repeal of the compact of 1820. Douglas led the van, and *Charles E. Stuart* followed as a volunteer to trample down the Missouri Compromise line, which was the last barrier to the unmolested spread of slavery toward the North. The free men of the North took up their abode in Kansas. At the first territorial election, the *pro-slavery border-ruffians of Missouri swarmed across the line*, took possession of the voting places, and drove the free voters away at the point of the bowie-knife and with pistols, at the expense of life and property. The national Democratic administretion, which was bound to afford protection to the actual settlers in Kansas, in their just rights, laughed at their cries for protection, and sent a standing army to drive back and annoy the settlers, and *protect and assist the intruding border-ruffians from Missouri* in their wicked depredations against liberty!

The Legislature thus elected, and composed of pro-slaveryites, actually residing in the State of Missouri, met and enacted the *most odious and oppressive Slavery Code that could be devised.* This was done under the protection of the Democratic party. When the people protested against their oppression, they were pointed to the bristling bayonets of the United States army, commanded by pro-slavery officers. We cannot stop to particularize the long catalogue of outrages and wrongs upon that people during 1855, 1856 and 1857. The history is familiar to the country. It was one continued series of outrages by the national Democratic administration party, through its willing officials, selected and appointed for the work. It would be a needless waste of words to recall to the public mind, the fraudulent election returns—the Kickapoo, Oxford, Delaware Crossing, and other glaring frauds upon the ballot boxes—by which *thousands* of pro-slavery votes were returned from precincts where there were not as many *dozens* of actual settlers. It is not necessary to recall the black-hearted and downright perjury of Calhoun and numerous other Democratic officials, or the "candle-box" operation, to rob the free men of Kansas of their rights, and force slavery upon them. We will not stop to rehearse the many acts of violence and bloodshed by slavery advocates, or the frauds of the "Lecompton Convention," which forged a pro-slavery Constitution. We will pass to the treachery of James Buchanan. He sent Gov. Walker to Kansas with positive instructions to tell the people they should have the opportunity of a *direct vote* upon the acceptance or rejection of any Constitution which the Convention might frame.

Walker, as well as Stanton, the Territorial Secretary, pledged the people of Kansas as instructed. When, subsequently, they attempted to execute their pledges, they were removed by Buchanan for doing so. The *whole power of the Government*, by Executive patronage and the National Treasury, was brought to bear *to force the odious Lecompton Slavery Constitution upon the people, without the privilege of a vote for or against it!!*

In this *wicked and infamous attempt to forge the chains of human slavery upon the energies of an unwilling people*, the Democratic party *set a price upon Liberty*, in a precedent that should arouse the indignation of every free voter of the North, whether of the Republican or Democratic party. The alarming precedent established was this: *They would admit Kansas as a State into the Union, with only* 35,000 *inhabitants, on condition that she would accept the infamous Lecompton Constitution, which established and protected* HUMAN SLAVERY, *IN ALL ITS BLIGHTING FORMS.* WHEREAS, if Kansas *refused* to thus submit to have a slavery constitution forced upon her, she *could not be admitted* until she obtained a population of 100,000! This is the price set upon freedom by the Democratic party. In this infamous foray upon the freedom of Kansas, the national expenditures have been run up to the alarming amount of one hundred and thirty-eight millions of dollars a year. We need not refer to the frauds, corruptions, *bribery*, of the last Congress to carry even the English-Lecompton bill through, which was but another form of the original and unadulterated "Lecompton," itself.

James Buchanan 29 Years Ago.

During the memorable contest of the Missouri Compromise, in the winter of 1819, a public meeting was held in Lancaster, Penn., the home of James Buchanan. He was then on the side of freedom. At that meeting, he was chairman of the committee to draft resolutions on the subject. He submitted the following:

"*Resolved*, That the Representatives in Congress from this district be, and they are hereby requested to use their utmost endeavor, as members of the National Legislature, to prevent the existence of slavery in any of the Territories or States which may be created by Congress."

[The second resolution requested the next Legislature to instruct the members of Congress from the entire State to do the same! Then iollowed]

"*Resolved*, That in the opinion of this meeting, the members of Congress who, at the last session, sustained the cause of justice, humanity and patriotism, in opposing the introduction of Slavery into the State then endeavoring to be formed out of the Missouri Territory, are entitled to the warmest thanks of every friend to humanity.

"*Resolved*, That the proceedings of this meeting be published in the newspapers of this city.

"JAMES BUCHANAN,
"JAMES HOPKINS,
"WM. JENKINS.

"The foregoing resolutions being read were unanimously adopted; after whieh the meeting adjourned. "WALTER FRANKLIN, *Ch'n.*

"*Attest*, WM. JENKINS, *Sec'y.*"

James Buchanan Now.

In 1856, James Buchanan endorsed the Cincinnati platform, which recognized "*the right* of the people of all the Territories, including Kansas and Nebraska, acting through the legally and fairly expressed *will of a majority* of actual inhabitants, to form a Constitution, with or without domestic slavery, and be admitted into the Union upon terms of perfect equality with the other States."

In 1857, James Buchanan, with cold-hearted affrontery, *denied* "the *right of the people*" to vote upon a constitution that said they *should* have slavery, although the "*fairly expressed will of a majority*" of more than ten thousand had repeatedly said they did not want a slavery constitution. It was here that James Buchanan, backed by the Democratic party, exerted the entire influence of his high position, and the money in the national treasury, to defeat the will of the majority, and force the Lecompton constitution upon them without allowing them a chance to vote it down!! Such is the Democratic policy. In beautiful contrast with his Lancaster resolutions of 1819, he said in his celebrated Kansas message, that "SLAVERY existed at that period (1854) and *still exists* IN KANSAS ☞ UNDER THE CONSTITUTION OF THE UNITED STATES. *This point has at last been FIRMLY DECIDED by the highest tribunal* (Judge Taney) *known to our laws.* How it COULD EVER HAVE BEEN DOUBTED *IS A MYSTERY.*"

And in his letter to Professor Sillman, he reiterated the above, and added, ☞ SLAVERY EXISTS IN KANSAS BY VIRTUE OF THE CONSTITUTION OF THE UNITED STATES. "☞ Kansas is, therefore, as much A SLAVE STATE as GEORGIA or SOUTH CAROLINA."

This simply shows Buchanan a quiet citizen of Pennsylvania, and Buchanan the President of the United States, a traitor to freedom, in the hands of the southern slave-breeders, ready to do their utmost bidding.

THE DEMOCRATIC STATUTES OF KANSAS.

That the free voters of Michigan may have a *faint idea* of what kind of a system the cohorts of slavery, through the Democratic party, with James Buchanan at its head, wished to forge upon the people of Kansas, without a privilege of voting against it, we subjoin the following mild extracts from the code which they prepared. How does it suit the tastes of the people of Michigan? Do they wish to *endorse* the efforts of the Democrats to force it down the throats of the people of Kansas, by voting for the Democratic State, Congressional, or County ticket?

"Sec. 6. If any person shall entice, decoy, "or carry out of any State or other Territory of "the United States, any slave belonging to an- "other, with intent to procure or effect the free- "dom of such slave, or to deprive the owner "thereof of the services of such slave, and shall "bring such slave into this Territory, he shall be "adjudged guilty of *grand larceny*, in the same "manner as if such slave shall have been brought "by such person, and on conviction thereof, the "person offending shall SUFFER DEATH, or "be imprisoned *at hard labor for not less than* "*ten years.*"

"Sec. 12. If any free person, by speaking or by "writing, shall assert or maintain that persons "have not the right to hold slaves in this Territory, "print, publish, write, circulate, or cause to be "introduced into this Territory, written, printed, "published or circulated in this Territory, any "book, paper, magazine, pamphlet or circular, "containing any denial of the right of persons to "hold slaves in this territory, such person shall "be deemed guilty of *felony*, and be punished by "imprisonment at hard labor for a term of not "less than two years."

"Sec. 13. No person who is conscientiously "opposed to holding slaves, or who does not ad- "mit the right to hold slaves in the territory, "shall sit as a juror, &c., &c"

Such is the *genius* of modern "Democracy" under its present corrupt leaders. The party stands convicted before the country of the most flagrant outrages upon the rights of the people. In our State, it has wantonly squandered the public funds for private uses, and grossly betrayed the confidence of the people who so long entrusted it with the affairs of the State. In the Nation, the same party has wantonly bankrupted the public Treasury in its extravagant and unholy efforts to spread the curse of human slavery over Free Territory. It has betrayed the rights of the people in denying those of Kansas the common and sacred privilege of choosing their own constitution. It has offered a reward for treason against the constitution, and the authority of the nation, by volunteering a free pardon to traitors, and is now using the peoples' money to shield the disgusting, demoralizing and heathenish sin of polygamy in the Territories of the United States! If not rebuked, the next foray of Democracy will be upon the Island of Cuba. for the sole and only purpose of adding a new *market* for human chattle to the territory of the Union. Human slavery is the pole-star of the Democratic party, as now organized. Its outrages upon Kanzas are only more proofs of its fixed policy.

It becomes every Free Voter of the North—to whatever party he may belong—to proclaim his disapprobation of this policy, through the legitimate means of the ballot box. This privilege is reserved to all. Let the ides of November proclaim to a corrupt slavery propogandins national administrational that the people of Michigan are indeed free—free to rebuke the wanton outrages upon the rights of their struggling brethren in Kansas, and free to roll on the car of liberty and equal rights.

☞ FREEMEN OF MICHIGAN!! — The most *important* issue now before you to decide at the approaching election, is *this one* of the policy of the National Democratic party towards Kansas, in the attempt to extend the dominion of slavery! The Democratic party asks your endorsement of all the wrongs towards Kansas, which we have but briefly alluded to. By voting the Democratic ticket you give your consent to these wrongs, as well as to the future attempts of the party to extend slavery, which now has *no barrier* to check its progress over free territory. Kansas is yet a territory, and her battle for freedom has *yet to be fought.* It may be in the next Congress—it may be in some future time. The South and the Democratic party have set a price upon freedom—*upon free States!* The price is a fearful one. *Vote for no doubtful champion of freedom.* No man *on the Democratic ticket*, surrounded with all the influences of party organization, *is safe on this question.* How often have the North been betrayed on this question by her chosen representatives of the Democratic party!!

People of Michigan—*who love freedom*—you are now called upon to place your solemn *seal of condemnation* upon the slavery policy of the Democratic party. You can only do so by voting against the regular nominations of that party. It is the only *effectual* way of saying to the wire-pullers that you do not approve of their riotings in the house of freedom. To make the rebuke emphatic and effective, vote against the whole ticket, from the lowest to the highest candidate. Your sentiments will not then be misunderstood. The people of Ohio, Indiana and Pennsylvania have just spoken on this subject. Indiana, which voted for Buchanan in 1856, has rebuked his wickedness. Ohio rolls up a majority of 25,000 against Lecompton. The people of *Pennsylvania*—Buchanan's own State—have wiped out "Democracy" and rebuked their once "favorite son" in the thundering tones of almost countless majorities against the participators in the Lecompton iniquities! ☞ Pennsylvania! which voted for Buchanan in 1856, now repudiates his policy by 40,000 or 50,000 majority!! Will the people of *Michigan* be less fearless, less patriotic? Let every voter for freedom be at the polls. Let Michigan strive with the Empire State, with Illinois and with freedom loving New England, for the largest majority for free soil, at the November elections.

By order of the
REPUBLICAN STATE CENTRAL COM.

www.ingramcontent.com/pod-product-compliance
Lightning Source LLC
La Vergne TN
LVHW020639110826
845149LV00004B/1289

* 9 7 8 1 4 1 8 1 9 0 4 5 3 *